FAT QUARTER
ONE–PIECE PROJECTS

FAT QUARTER
ONE–PIECE
PROJECTS

25 projects to make from short lengths of fabric

Tina Barrett

First published 2018 by
Guild of Master Craftsman Publications Ltd
Castle Place, 166 High Street, Lewes,
East Sussex, BN7 1XU

ISBN 978 1 78494 420 9

A catalogue record for this book is available from the British Library.

Publisher Jonathan Bailey
Production Jim Bulley and Jo Pallett
Senior Project Editor Dominique Page
Editor Robin Pridy
Managing Art Editor Gilda Pacitti
Design & Art Direction Wayne Blades
Photographer Neal Grundy
Step photography Jeff Barrett

Colour origination by GMC Reprographics

Printed and bound in China

A note on measurements
The imperial measurements in these projects are converted from metric. While every attempt has been made to ensure that they are as accurate as possible, some rounding up or down has been inevitable. For this reason, it is always best to stick to one system or the other throughout a project: do not mix metric and imperial units.

CONTENTS

INTRODUCTION

When I was asked to design a book of projects using a single fat quarter I was thrilled because, as anyone who sews or crafts knows, we always have multiple fat quarters or small amounts of fabric left over from larger projects. But what to do with them? They are invariably far too lovely to throw away but on the other hand, the stash box is already bulging! So this book was very timely but also a challenge. The brief was tight. I was to use one fat quarter only plus lining and embellishments, which, in all fairness, is what we are usually faced with within our own stash.

My goal was to create 25 gorgeous projects that could be displayed and used around the house or, alternatively, given as fabulous gifts that anybody might be thrilled to receive. I hope I have succeeded and that you are inspired to create a few of my fat quarter projects and use up some of your own fabric stash too.

The book is divided into five sections to fit your home: Kitchen/Diner, Living Room, Office/Workroom, Bedroom and Nursery. I have kept the techniques very simple so you will only need basic sewing skills and a sewing machine. A fat quarter usually measures 18 x 22in (46 x 56cm) and is cut from the bolt and then cut in half again. Occasionally, I use a long fat quarter when the project suits. This measures 10 x 44in (25 x 112cm) and is cut using the full width of the bolt. As long as you are using the correct size, the colour and pattern choice are completely up to you.

So there you have it, the perfect excuse to get your machine out and use up that fabric you've been eyeing up for months (or in my case, even years!) and create something special. And when you've created a hole in your stash, it will, of course, need to be refilled...

Tina B x

THE BASICS

MATERIALS & EQUIPMENT

Most of the projects in this book can be made using one fat quarter and a very small, basic toolkit. In fact, you probably already have many of these items in your home. The only extras you will need are a staple gun and a lampshade kit.

SCISSORS You will need a good-quality set of dressmaking shears, a small sharp pair for hand sewing and nipping off thread plus a general pair for cutting out paper templates. Avoid using your best fabric shears for paper, which will blunt the blades. Pinking shears are really useful for preventing fraying or to add a decorative effect to your work. The triangular-shaped blade gives a pretty zigzag edge to the fabric as you cut it.

SEAM RIPPER & PINS This tool is very useful for unpicking stitches. Simply insert the tip under the first stitch and press it forwards against the curved blade. Large coloured heads on pins can be much easier to find, and don't get lost in the seams. Use safety pins for threading elastic or tape through casings.

NEEDLES Sharp hand-sewing needles are a must for closing holes left for stuffing or turning. Embroidery needles are thicker with a bigger eye for embroidery thread and it is wise to keep a few spare sewing-machine needles that work for the type of fabric you are sewing.

QUILTER'S FABRIC SPRAY GLUE Used most frequently by quilters, this spray glue is essential when working with wadding and linings.

MEASURING TAPES & RULERS These are invaluable in a sewing room. A large plastic measure incorporating curves, straight edges and seam allowance guides, can also be helpful. I have included both metric and imperial measurements throughout the book. To maintain accuracy, remember not to mix the two.

MARKERS, COMPASS & PAPER Disappearing fabric markers are perfect for when you are not sure of a mark or measurement. They fade after a few minutes, giving you enough time to stitch along your drawn guideline. Tailor's chalk is cheap and readily available. It has a sharp end to accurately mark lines onto your fabric and the powder can be brushed off afterwards. For the templates in the book, a basic pen, pencil, compass and paper set is ideal and gives you the means to resize your project if required.

FABRICS Most of the projects in this book are made from cotton fabric that is suitable for dressmaking or quilting. Calico is an ideal, inexpensive lining choice – the ecru colour blends in with most pattern choices.

INTERFACING/STABILIZERS Interfacing acts as a stabilizer to support fabric and will help your project keep its shape – a thick weight can even enable the fabric to stand up without support, such as the trinket dish on page 96. For most of the projects in this book, a lightweight interfacing is all that is required. Fusible interfacing has a layer of glue on one side that sticks to the surface of your fabric when heat is applied.

THREADS & HABERDASHERY As most of the projects' fabrics are cotton, it is preferable to also use cotton thread – this allows fabric and thread to wash well together without fading or shrinking. For an invisible finish, choose a thread colour to match your fabric. Or, choose a colour contrast to give your piece an extra dimension. Zips, too, can be invisible, or you can add a colour pop or feature a charm on the pull tag. Other haberdashery, such as buttons, lace, bells and felt, can add a special touch. It is always worth having plenty of these to hand, but be sure to choose the correct length and weight for your project.

STUFFING For filling toys and accessories, or providing padding, regular polyester toy stuffing works best, as it is allergy free, light and washable. You can also use wool or scraps of fabric if you prefer. To add weight to a project you are stuffing, you need something a bit heavier than polyester or wool. Nearly any type of dried pulse or rice will work for this but it must be really dry to avoid becoming mouldy over time. An extra pair of hands is useful at filling time or, failing that, a plastic funnel helps you pour and avoid spillage.

NOTE

Don't forget these essentials – they don't need to be fancy, as long as they work:

SEWING MACHINE
BOBBINS Make sure you keep a few loaded up in your most used/favourite colours so they are quick and handy to change over when needed.
IRON & IRONING BOARD

TECHNIQUES

All the projects in this book can be created with very simple stitches using a sewing machine and hand stitching. Refer to this handy guide when tackling a new technique.

PREPARING TO SEW

Take a moment or two to read through the whole of the project notes before assembling all the tools and materials you will need. Take time to prepare any templates and remember to check twice before cutting your fabric. Press between steps wherever possible as it helps to keep work crisp and sharp.

USING TEMPLATES

Some of the projects require a template from the back of the book, or ask for you to make one using circles, squares or rectangles. Use tracing paper to make a copy first. If it needs enlarging, you can do this easily on a photocopier. For regular shapes such as a square or rectangle, use a ruler and fabric marker directly onto the wrong side of the fabric but remember to keep things square with the pattern repeat on your chosen fabric.

MARKING FABRIC

When specific measurements are given or if you would like to add embroidery to your project, it is best to make a mark directly onto the fabric. Use a disappearing fabric marker, where the ink starts to go when exposed to the air so that by the time you have finished stitching, the pen marks are already fading. Or, for darker fabrics, use tailor's chalk, which comes in various colours. Mine is flat and triangular to achieve an accurate mark. The chalk brushes off after sewing.

HAND SEWING

RUNNING STITCH

This simple stitch is prefect for tacking, gathering fabric, stabilizing curves or as a decorative flourish. You may wish to use a disappearing fabric marker to draw a line along where you'd like your running stitch to go, especially to achieve a decorative finish. Thread your needle and make a knot in the end of the thread. You can work long, medium or short stitches depending on how you'd like everything to look.

Begin by making a straight stitch to your preferred length. Bring the needle through from the back of the work to the front and then

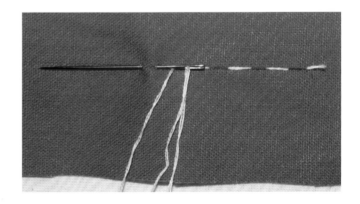

down again from front to back. Repeat this step, leaving an even space between stitches and keep following your line until you reach the end. Fasten off by making a few small stitches on the back of your work and snipping the thread.

SLIPSTITCH

This works well for closing an opening after turning it right side out, as most of the thread is hidden inside the work so it doesn't show on the outside of the work.

1 Work from right to left and with the needle pointing to the left. Anchor the thread and slip the needle through the folded edge of the hem and bring through to the right side of the work. As the needle comes out of the hem, slide the tip of the needle inside the opposite hem for about ³⁄₈in (1cm).

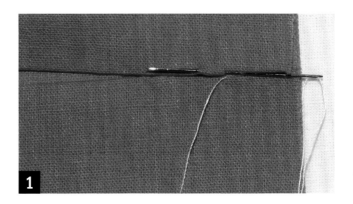

2 As the needle comes out of the fabric, slide the needle tip inside the hem of the first hem for ³⁄₈in (1cm) as in step 1. To create the next stitch, slip the needle back inside the hem where the previous stitch ended. Repeat steps 1 and 2.

SEWING ON A BUTTON

1 With your thread doubled, tie a knot in the end and pull your needle to the front of the fabric and through the first hole of the button.

2 Pass the needle down through the opposite hole and to the back of the fabric. Pass the needle up and down through the holes several more times. If there are four holes, make a cross shape by working opposite hole to opposite hole. Fasten off by making a few small stitches on the back of the work and snipping the thread.

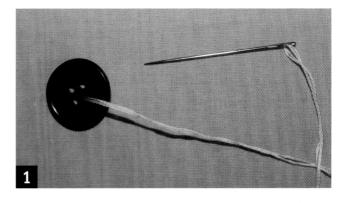

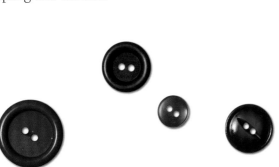

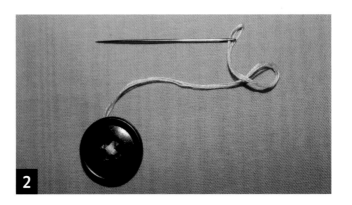

BACKSTITCH

This is a simple first embroidery stitch for outlining shapes and features.

1 You may wish to use a disappearing fabric marker to draw a line along where you'd like your backstitch to go, especially if it is to achieve a decorative finish. Thread your needle and make a knot in the end of the thread. Anchor it at the back of your work in the place you'd like to start. Make a single, straight stitch as long or as short as you want. Mine are usually about ¼in (6mm) long.

2 Continue along your pattern line but come up a space ahead.

3 Bring your needle back down into the same hole as the end of the last stitch you made. Repeat steps 2 and 3 until you reach the end. Fasten off by making a few small stitches on the back of the work and snipping the thread.

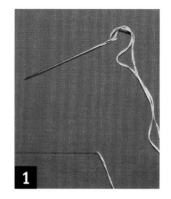
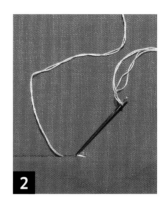
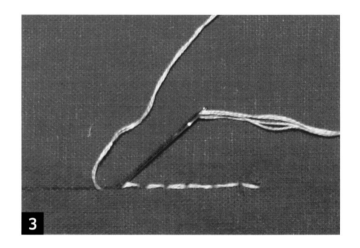

MACHINE SEWING

Choose a table that is the correct height for you to sit comfortably and work the machine without slumping. If you don't have a window, a good lamp will provide the light you need. Before you begin, be sure to thread the needle and bobbin correctly for your machine, choosing the right thread and needle size for your project. A needle threader can make life easier when threading up the eye of the machine needle.

Set the stitch length and width according to the project you are completing. Try stitching a spare piece of fabric to see if the tension is correct before moving onto your precious cut fabric. If you are unsure of how to set the tension or stitch length/width on your machine, take time to consult the manual before beginning.

TOPSTITCHING

Topstitching is a line of straight machine stitches worked on the right side of the fabric. It can be worked in a contrast colour for detail or can be matched for a sharp but invisible finish. It is also used to attach pieces such as straps.

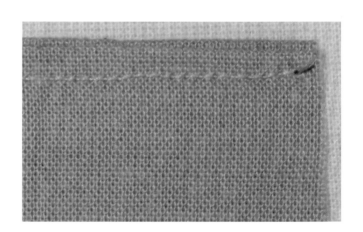

KITCHEN/ DINER

CHILD'S APRON

Make this sweet apron for the junior chef in your life and you'll find it easier to get help in the kitchen! It's such a simple make, you'll run it up in an afternoon. You'll need just one fat quarter of fabric, a pair of cute buttons and some good-quality tape for the ties.

Finished size is roughly:
20in (50cm) wide x 18in (47cm) long

You will need
1 fat quarter of fabric
60in (1.5m) of tape for ties
2 decorative buttons
Disappearing fabric marker
Sewing machine
Matching thread
Pins
Dressmaking scissors
Tape measure
Iron and ironing board
Sewing needle

NOTE: This project uses the whole of one fat quarter.

Tip
If you have any spare contrast fabric left over from other projects, you could add a decorative pocket to the front. It would also look cute with the addition of some ric-rac.

1 Making sure your fabric pattern is the right way up, fold the fabric in half lengthways and mark with a fabric pen 4in (10cm) along the top from the folded side and 9in (23cm) down. Draw a diagonal line joining these two marks and cut across the corner.

2 Fold a ³⁄₈in (1cm) hem twice around all sides. Press and then topstitch in place (see page 16) using a sewing machine.

3 For the straps, cut two lengths of tape about 18in (46cm) long and machine stitch them to each side of the wrong side of the apron at the waist.

4 Fold the raw edges of the waist straps over at the free end and machine stitch in place to prevent fraying.

5 For the neck strap, cut another piece of tape approximately 16in (41cm) long and machine stitch to one side on the wrong side at the top of the apron. Repeat for the opposite side. You may want to try the apron on your apron wearer to make sure the length is correct before sewing the second side.

6 Sew the two decorative buttons to the front of the apron where the neck strap is attached. You could also add a pocket or some decorative ric-rac or ribbon.

Tip

For a more robust, wipe-clean apron, you could use oilcloth.

1

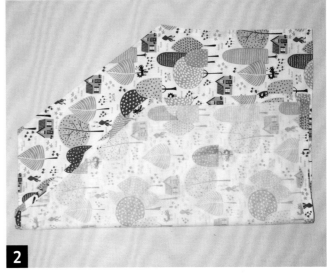
2

3

4

5

6

TRIVET

A good trick to jazz up a simple project is to add a contrast edging. I've used bias binding to pep up this functional trivet, which is perfect because the natural stretch of the binding follows the curve of the trivet beautifully.

Finished size is roughly:
8½in (22cm) diameter

You will need
1 fat quarter of fabric
1 piece of wadding big enough to make a 9in (23cm) circle
40in (1m) of contrast bias binding
Fabric spray glue
Sewing machine
Matching thread
Decorative button (optional)
Sewing needle
Iron and ironing board
Pins
Dressmaking scissors
Disappearing fabric marker
Compass, pencil and paper to make a template
    or a 9in (23cm) diameter plate
Paper-cutting scissors (if making a template)

NOTE: You could use the same material for the lining as there will be enough left over from the fat quarter.

Tip

*For a more decorative effect,
you could quilt over the fabrics
before applying the bias binding.*

1 Using the compass and pencil, draw a 9in (23cm) circle on a piece of paper. Cut this out and use as a template for your trivet. Alternatively, draw around a 9in (23cm) plate if you have one. Cut two pieces of fabric and one piece of wadding.

2 Place the bottom piece wrong side up onto a flat surface. Put the wadding on top followed by the top piece of fabric with right side facing upwards. Use fabric spray glue to stick the layers together with the wadding in the middle. Machine stitch closely around the edge to secure all the layers. Trim excess.

3 Open up one folded edge of the bias binding and pin in place around the edge of the trivet. Overlap the ends of the binding by about 1in (2.5cm), trimming on the diagonal. Machine stitch in place along the crease of the binding. Trim excess.

4 Fold the bias binding around the raw edge and press. Pin in place.

5 Using a sewing needle and thread, slipstitch (see page 15) in place. Leave a small opening for the loop but leave the needle and thread attached.

6 Fold 2in (5cm) of bias binding in half to make a loop and slip inside the open edge of the binding. Finish hand stitching the binding and loop into place. Then fold the loop upwards, press and secure with a few small hand stitches. Add a decorative button if you wish.

Tip

You could use a sewing machine to stitch the back of the bias binding instead of hand sewing if you prefer.

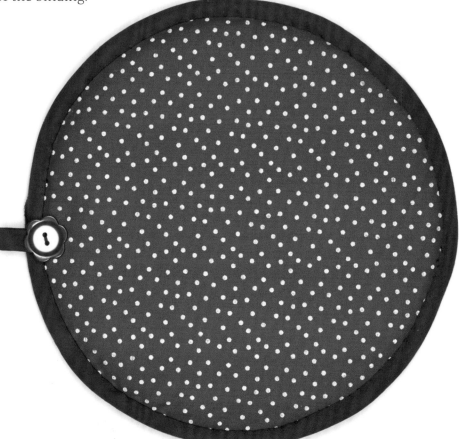

1 Fold the main fabric in half and use the template on page 130 to cut out two pieces of main fabric, lining and wadding. By folding the fabric first, you will have two mirror images of the glove: the back and the front. Cut one 3in (7.5cm) piece of bias binding or ribbon for a hanging loop.

2 Spray the wrong side of both pieces of main fabric with fabric spray glue and place the wadding on top. Spray the wadding and place the lining on top. You now have two sandwiches of fabric making up the front and back of the oven glove.

3 Place the pieces together, right sides facing. Fold the hanging loop in half and slide it into the side seam near the bottom edge and on the opposite side to the thumb. Machine stitch around the outside edges using a ³⁄₈in (1cm) seam allowance. Leave the bottom open.

4 Trim the excess fabric from the seam right down to the base of the thumb. Turn the rights sides out. Press.

5 Pin the bias binding around the outside of the bottom edge of the glove, overlapping the short ends by 1in (2.5cm). Machine stitch along the crease.

6 Fold the binding downwards and then up inside the wrong side of the glove. Using a sewing needle and thread, slipstitch (see page 15) in place.

Tip

Fabric spray glue makes life a lot easier – it secures layers without the need for pinning or tacking.

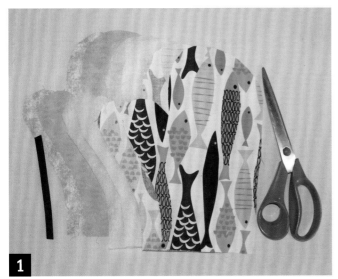

1

2

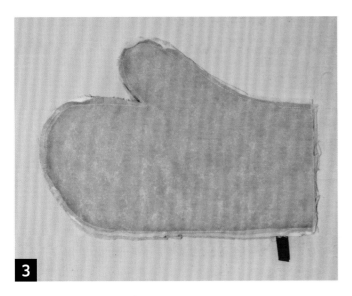

3

4

5

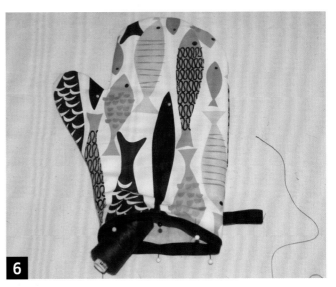

6

BAR STOOL COVER

This is such a great way to upcycle an everyday stool. By making a removable seat cover, you can update the furniture every single time you change the decor in your home, or you could make several covers in different colours and patterns to ring the changes!

Finished size is roughly:
11½in (29cm) diameter

You will need
1 fat quarter of main fabric
1 fat quarter of lining fabric
1 circle of wadding 13in (33cm) in diameter
  (or actual diameter of your stool top)
Paper, pen and compass for drawing a template
60in (1.5m) drawstring
60in (1.5m) of bias binding
Dressmaking scissors
Paper-cutting scissors
Pins
Safety pin
Tape measure
Sewing machine
Matching thread
Fabric spray glue
Iron and ironing board
Ruler
Disappearing fabric marker

NOTE: If you don't want to fiddle with tying a drawstring, you could insert elastic inside the casing instead. Using the head of a safety pin, push the elastic through the length of the casing until it pops out effortlessly at the opposite end.

LIVING ROOM

PHOTO FRAME

Photo frames can add a lovely accent to any room. It is very easy to personalize an inexpensive frame by adding a quirky piece of fabric and giving it a designer look. You could also embellish the fabric by sewing on buttons or sequins.

Finished size is roughly:
6¾in (17cm) wide x 8¾in (22cm) high

You will need
1 fat quarter of fabric
1 fat quarter of wadding
1 x 4 x 6in (10 x 15cm) photo frame with a flat (not bevelled) border on the front
Staple or glue gun
Fabric spray glue
Disappearing fabric marker
Ruler or tape measure
Pins
Dressmaking scissors
Small sharp scissors

NOTE: If you don't own a hot glue gun or staple gun, very strong glue will do just as well.

Tip
A craft knife can be very handy for trimming the excess fabric around the inner edge of the photo frame centre.

1 Using the compass, draw a circle for the base and a rectangle for the sides onto tracing paper and cut out to make patterns. A large bucket has a base diameter of 7½in (19cm) and an 11 x 21½in (28 x 55cm) rectangle. Seam allowances of ⅜in (1cm) are included. Cut out one piece each of main fabric, lining and stabilizer for each piece.

2 Iron the main fabric of the base and the rectangle to the stabilizer pieces.

3 With right sides facing, using a ⅜in (1cm) seam allowance, pin and machine sew the lining to the main fabric along the top long edge of the rectangle. Open out and press.

4 Fold the rectangle piece in half, lengthwise, with right sides facing together, so that each side is part outer and part lining. With a ⅜in (1cm) seam allowance, pin the long side to form a cylinder. Machine sew the main fabric edge, then carry on for 1½in (4cm) along the lining before leaving a 4in (10cm) gap and continuing to sew all the way to the end. This gap is the opening to turn the basket through when it is completed.

5 Pin the fabric bases in place: the lining base to the cylinder's lined edge, right sides together; and the main fabric base to the main fabric end, right sides together. Machine stitch in place with a ⅜in (1cm) seam allowance. Trim the seams (see page 18) and carefully clip notches around the circle (see page 18).

6 Turn the basket through the open section of the lining's side seam. With right sides out, slipstitch (see page 15) the side seam opening closed. To form the basket, push the lining into the outer fabric. Topstitch (see page 16) round the top edge. Fold down the top for a contrast edge.

Tip

If you are having trouble deciding what colour lining to use, it's a good idea to look for one of the colours that feature in the pattern of your main fabric.

1

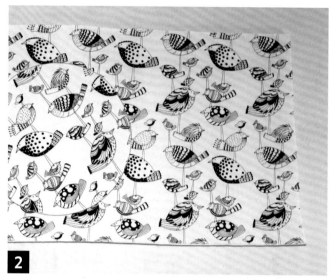

2

3

4

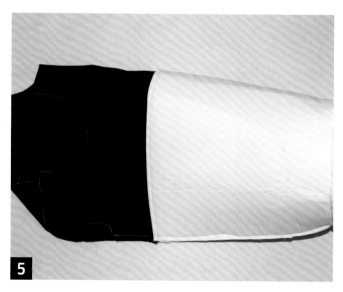

5

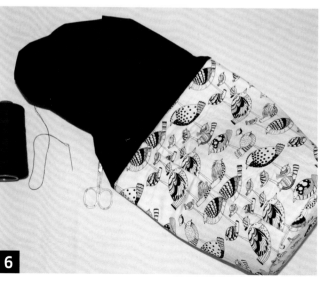

6

MAGAZINE RACK

If you have a glossy magazine addiction like I have, then you'll want to store them tidily so they are handy to browse whenever you have a quiet five minutes. This magazine rack is the perfect solution and will hang neatly behind a door or on the wall.

Finished size is roughly:
9¾in (25cm) wide x 17in (43cm) high

You will need
1 fat quarter of main fabric
1 fat quarter of lining fabric
1 fat quarter of fusible interfacing
Contrast bias binding
1 length of dowel
Ruler or tape measure
Pins
Disappearing fabric marker
Sewing machine
Matching thread
Dressmaking scissors
Sewing needle
Iron and ironing board

NOTE: You don't have to use dowel to hang this project. You could buy a large eyelet set and attach them to the top edge then use wall hooks to hang it up instead.

1 Cut out the back piece of the rack: one piece each of main fabric, lining and interfacing, to 10½ x 18in (27 x 46cm). Cut out the front pocket: one piece of main fabric and lining, to 10½ x 11in (27 x 28cm).

2 Assemble the pocket. Place lining and main fabric together with right sides facing. Machine stitch across the top short edge using a ³⁄₈in (1cm) seam allowance. Open out and press.

3 Fold the lining to the wrong side of the pocket. Add some decorative bias binding or ric-rac to the pocket if you like. I have topstitched a contrast piece just below the top edge. Pin and machine stitch the decoration into place.

4 Iron fusible interfacing to the main fabric of the back piece. Press a ³⁄₈in (1cm) seam to the wrong sides of the top edge of the back piece. Do the same for the lining.

5 Make a sandwich by placing the back piece on a flat surface with right side facing upwards. Place the pocket on next at the bottom of the back piece and with the right side facing upwards. Now place the lining on top with right side facing downwards.

6 Measure down 1in (2.5cm) from the top edge on both sides and mark with marker. Pin and machine stitch from this point down around the long edge, across the bottom and up the second long side to the second mark.

7 Turn right sides out and press. To make a dowel channel, topstitch (see page 16) the open top seam (you pressed the seams neatly inwards in step 4) along its edge.

8 Mark a line ½in (12mm) below the topstitched seam at the top. Topstitch along this line to create a dowel channel. Cut the dowel to length so that there is a 2in (5cm) piece protruding from each end. Add a loop of ribbon at each end or simply rest the dowel on a pair of hooks, as shown on page 53.

Tip

If you want to add multiple pockets, just use more fabric and make the backing piece longer. Add as many pockets as you like.

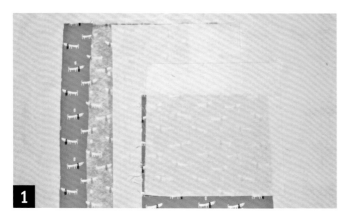

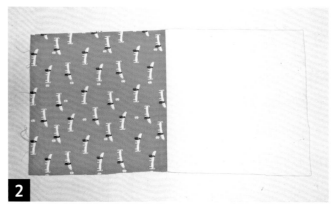

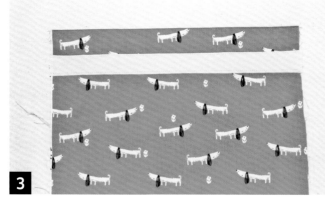

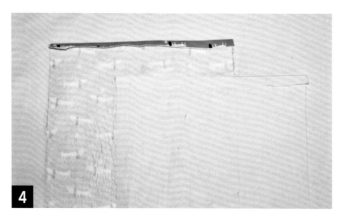

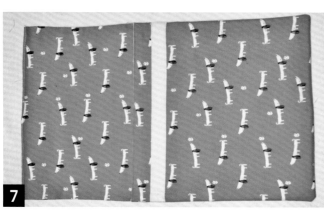

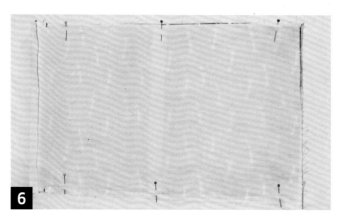

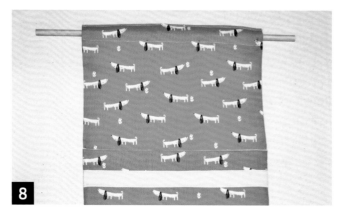

CUSHION

If you love Sashiko embroidery, then this cushion is a great first project on which to practise the technique. The simple running stitches add texture and interest to the plain linen base, while the tassels and contrast lining fabric bring a touch of luxury.

Finished size is roughly:
14in (35cm) square

You will need
1 fat quarter of linen
1 fat quarter of red lining fabric
4 tassels (optional)
Red embroidery thread
Embroidery needle
14 x 14in (36 x 36cm) cushion pad
14 x 14in (36 x 36cm) piece of wadding
Sewing machine
Matching thread
Dressmaking scissors
Disappearing fabric marker
Ruler
Pins
Iron and ironing board

NOTE: The front of the cushion takes a whole fat quarter, so you will need a contrast/matching lining for the back piece.

Tip
Instead of the straight stitches shown here, you could try drawing circles of different sizes across the cushion front and embroidering around the edges.

1 Cut out the top piece of the cushion – 14½ x 14½in (37.5 x 37.5cm) in linen and also in wadding. Now cut two pieces of red lining, each 9 x 14½in (23.5cm x 37.5cm).

2 Press the top piece of linen and, using a ruler and disappearing fabric marker, draw vertical lines across the width of the piece approximately ¾in (2cm) apart leaving a 2in (5cm) border around the edge. Pin the wadding to the wrong side of the linen around the edges and through the centre.

3 Use two strands of embroidery thread held together and an embroidery needle and work a line of small running stitches by hand (see page 14), along every straight line, working through both linen and wadding to give a padded look.

4 Take one of the pieces of red lining. Press a ³⁄₈in (1cm) hem along the long edge. Turn under again by another ³⁄₈in (1cm), press and then topstitch (see page 16) close to the edge. Repeat for the second piece.

5 Place the embroidered piece onto a flat surface with the right side facing upwards. Place the tassels at each corner with the loops pointing outermost. Put the two red lining pieces on top, as shown, with the centre pieces overlapping, and pin securely all around the edges.

6 Using a ⁵⁄₈in (1.5cm) seam allowance, stitch around all four edges. Turn the cushion cover right side out and insert the cushion pad.

Tip

Tape the raw edges of the linen base with masking tape to prevent fraying while you embroider.
It peels off afterwards and prevents the edges from getting tatty.

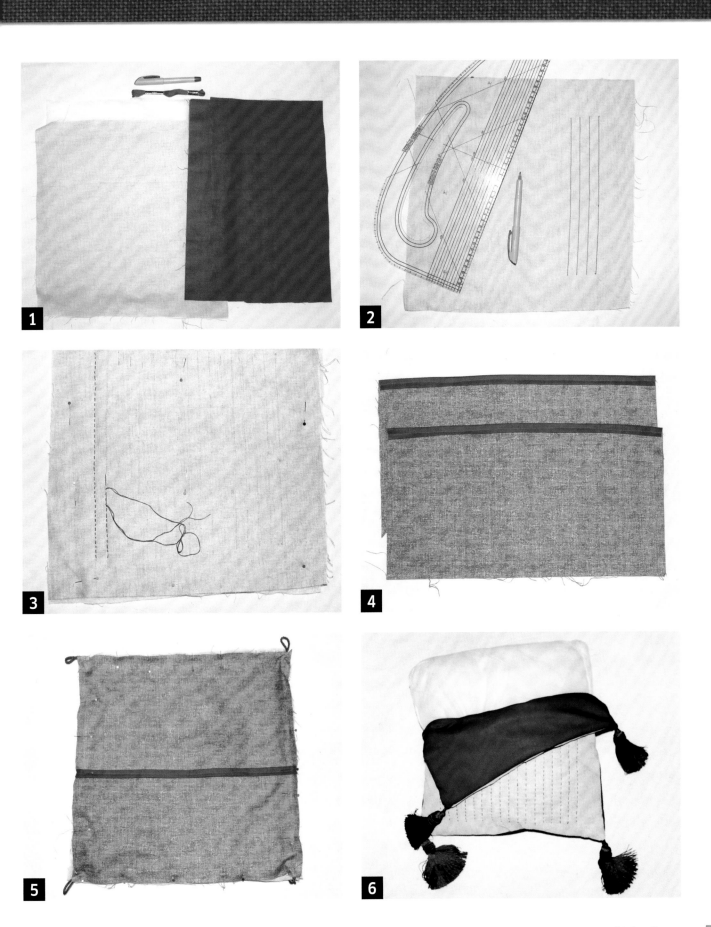

OFFICE/ WORKROOM

PINBOARD

This useful pinboard is the perfect addition to your office. Using just one fat quarter and an inexpensive art canvas, you can keep all your notes, inspiration and schedules right where you can see them. Why not make a couple so you can keep one for family events?

Finished size is roughly:
12in (31cm) square

You will need
Art canvas, 12 x 12in (30 x 30cm)
1 fat quarter of fabric
Wadding
Staple gun
Fabric spray glue
11 matching buttons
Sewing needle and matching thread
Disappearing fabric marker
Matching elastic/ribbon
Tape/bias binding to neaten the back (optional)
Dressmaking scissors

NOTE: If you hate sewing on buttons, a hot glue gun will also secure them in place without the tears.

Tip
Use some bias binding or webbing across the back edges just to neaten things up. Secure in place with a staple gun or a hot glue gun.

1 Place the canvas in the centre of the fabric and mark the outline on the wrong side with a disappearing fabric marker.

2 Cut a piece of wadding 12 x 12in (30 x 30cm). Use fabric spray glue to fix it in place to the art canvas.

3 Using your previous marks as a guide, place the canvas and wadding face down onto the wrong side of the fabric. Fold in the edges to neaten, then staple along one side.

4 Repeat for the other three sides, tightening the fabric as you go.

5 Turn the board right side up and lay out the elastic/ribbon, forming a diamond pattern.

6 Secure the ribbons at the back using staples and trim any excess.

7 Turn the board right side up and sew a button through all thicknesses, including the canvas, at the point where each diamond crosses.

8 If you wish, you can neaten the back by stapling tape around the frame or merely trim the excess fabric.

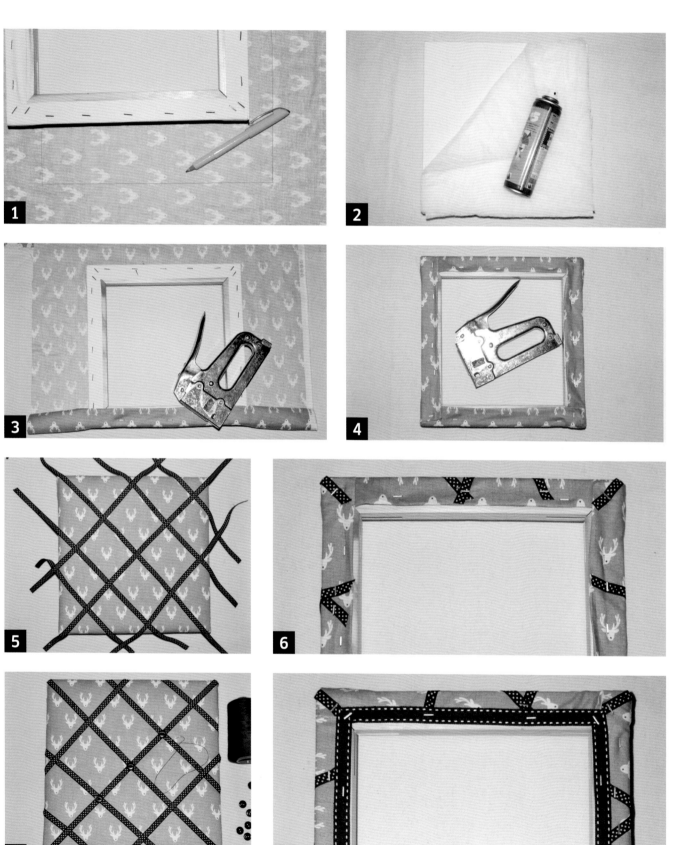

WRIST CUSHIONS

If you spend much of your day slaving over a keyboard then this is just the project to save your wrists from dreaded repetitive strain. These simple wrist cushions are easy and inexpensive to make and will help ensure your deadlines never run over time.

Finished sizes are roughly:
Keyboard cushion – 5in (13cm) wide x 16in (40cm) long
Mouse cushion – 3¾in (10cm) square

You will need
1 fat quarter of fabric
2lb (1kg) bag rice or dried peas
Funnel
Tape measure or ruler
Pins
Dressmaking scissors
Iron and ironing board
Sewing machine
Matching thread

NOTE: You may need an extra pair of hands to help pour your rice into the cushion covers as it is a little tricky. If you don't have this luxury, pop the open bag into a large bowl so any spillages will be safely caught.

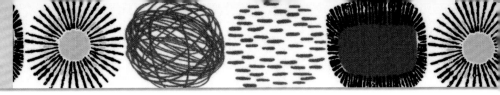

1 Cut out two 5½ x 9½in (14 x 24cm) pieces each in both lining and main fabric. Fold down a ⅜in (1cm) hem on one long side of each piece and press.

2 With one of the main fabric pieces and one lining piece, make a zip sandwich with the folded edges close to the zip's teeth. The lining should be at the bottom with the right side face down. The zip comes next with the main fabric on top with the right side facing uppermost. Pin in place.

3 Machine stitch the pieces together. A zipper foot can be useful for getting in close to the zip's teeth and making a nice, secure seam. Repeat for the opposite side.

4 Place the right sides of the main fabric together and machine stitch the remaining long seam closed through all four layers, using a ⅝in (1.5cm) seam allowance. Trim the excess away.

5 With wrong side facing out, flatten the pouch so the zip sits directly above the bottom seam. Now machine stitch across both short edges using a ⅝in (1.5cm) seam allowance. Stitch across all layers including the zip ends. Trim the excess.

6 Turn the case right sides out so that the zipper sits in the middle. You can leave it just like this for a flat, wide-style case or you can box the corners to make it more cube-like as follows.

7 To box each corner (see page 18), turn the wrong side out and flatten one short edge. Use your marker to draw across the corner. Mark each line about 1½–2in (4–5cm) wide across every corner.

8 Machine stitch across each line in all four corners. Trim to neaten and reduce bulk. Turn the case right side out.

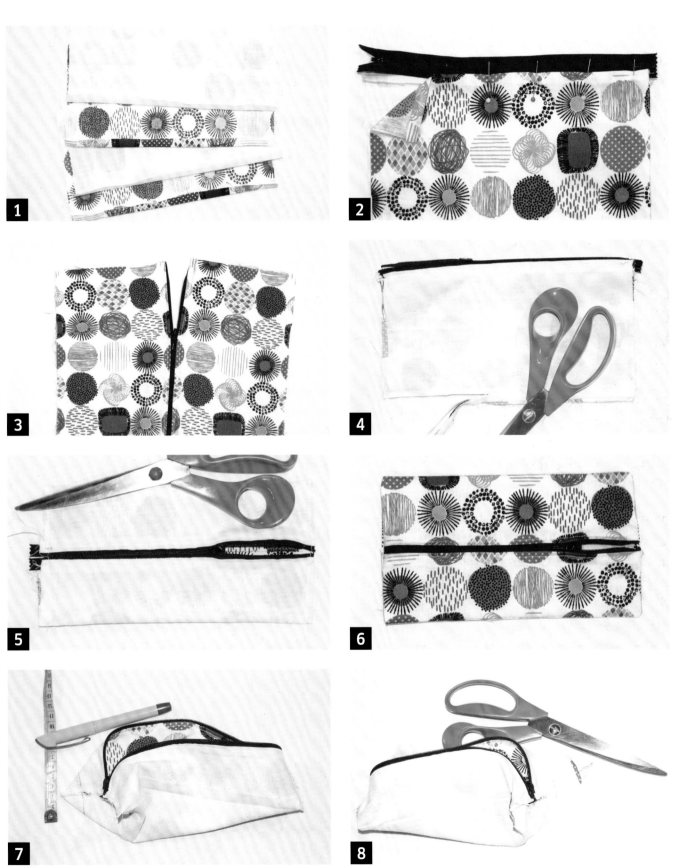

COVERED NOTEBOOK

Jazz up your 'to do' lists with this bright notebook cover. You could use a contrast lining so the inside of the pocket flaps coordinate, or even clash, with the main fabric. I've used a decorative button tab for a closure but you could add a ribbon or coloured elastic.

Finished size is roughly:
6in (15cm) wide x 8½in (21cm) high

You will need
1 fat quarter of fabric
1 fat quarter of lining fabric
Fusible interfacing
1 decorative button
1 snap fastener
Sewing machine
Dressmaking scissors
Disappearing fabric marker
Pins
Iron and ironing board
Sewing needle and matching thread
Tape measure
1 A5 hardback notebook

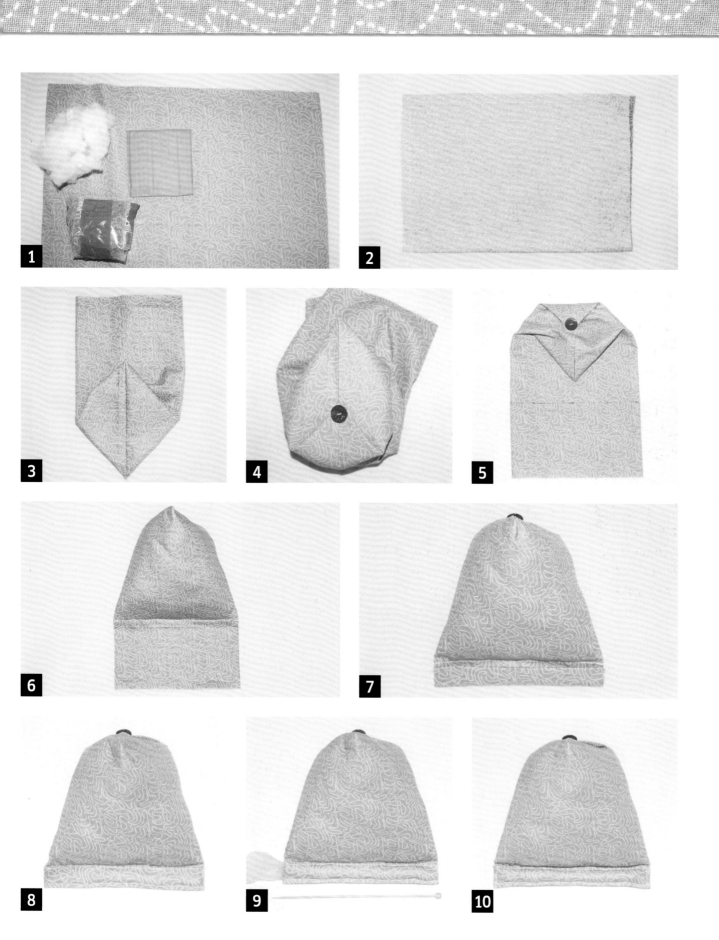

BEDROOM

SLEEP MASK

Enjoy a power nap or a quick snooze every now and then? Sleep in style and block out distractions with this comfortable and pretty, easy-to-make eye mask. If you are feeling creative, you could embroider eyelashes onto the front of the eye mask.

Finished size is roughly:
10½in (27cm) wide x 3½in (8.5cm) high

Find the template on page 131

You will need
1 fat quarter of main fabric
1 fat quarter of lining fabric
1 fat quarter of wadding
22in (56cm) of elastic
Tape measure
Tracing paper and pen
Dressmaking scissors
Paper-cutting scissors
Pins
Sewing machine
Matching thread
Sewing needle
Iron and ironing board

Tip

If you don't like the look of the elastic, you could make a long casing out of contrast material and thread the elastic through the centre to disguise it. Use the head of a safety pin to push the elastic through the length of the casing until it pops out the other end.

1 The templates in this book is for a UK size 5–7 (US 7.5–9.5, EU 38.5–41). If your foot is a different size, make your own templates by placing your foot on a piece of card and drawing around it. Remove your foot and add a ¾in (2cm) seam allowance to the outer edge of this shape. Cut out the shape to make the sole. Draw a line across the width of the foot about halfway down. Place the foot template onto another piece of card and extend the outside of the top half by 1in (2.5cm). Cut out this shape to make the upper.

2 Cut one piece of fabric, wadding and lining from both shapes. Flip the templates to make a mirror image and repeat the process.

3 For the first slipper top, place the fabric on top of the wadding, right side up. Then place the lining on top with the wrong side upwards. Machine stitch across the straight edge, trim excess, turn it right side out and press. Repeat these steps for the second slipper. If you want to attach ribbon or ric-rac (see picture), stitch it on now. I have machine stitched mine but you could also hand stitch it.

4 For the bases, place the fabric, wadding and lining into a sandwich for both sets of pieces, so that the main fabric is facing right side up. Secure with fabric spray glue.

5 For the first slipper, pin one of the bases to one of the slipper tops and machine stitch all around the outside close to the edge to secure all the layers together. Repeat for second slipper.

6 Pin bias binding all around the edge of both slippers, overlapping the edges by 1in (2.5cm). Machine stitch in the crease. Trim excess and clip notches into the curves (see page 18).

7 For both slippers, fold to the underside, pin and hand sew the bias binding in place using slipstitch (see page 15).

Tip

Avoid extra work by drawing out only one template. Simply flip the template over to cut out the second foot.

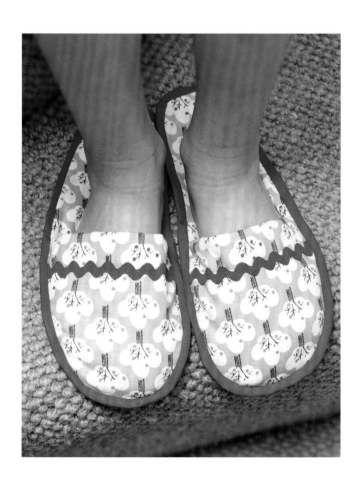

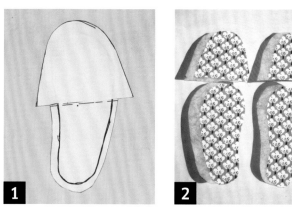

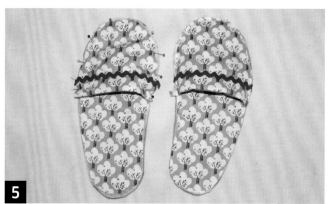

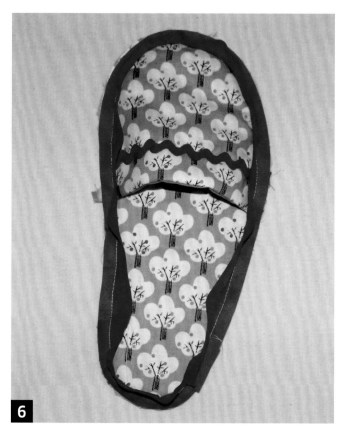

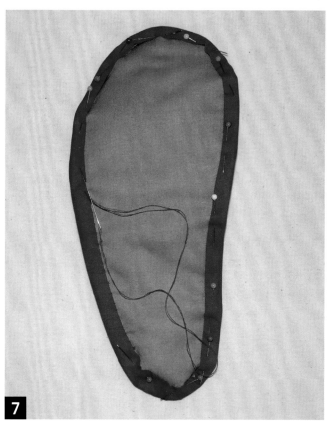

1

2

3

4

5

6

7

LAMPSHADE

Using a simple lampshade kit and an inexpensive fat quarter you can create statement lighting to complement any room. This lampshade makes a lovely, cosy bedside light. You could add braid or a fringe to the edges to give it a more luxurious look.

Finished size is roughly:
8in (20cm) diameter x 7½in (19cm) high

You will need
1 long fat quarter (see page 8)
1 x 8in (20cm) lampshade kit
Sharp scissors
Iron and ironing board
Fabric spray glue and braid or fringing (optional)

Tip
Instead of using a lampshade kit, why not search thrift stores for an inexpensive old lampshade that you can reuse?

1 Cut two 10 x 20in (25 x 50cm) pieces of main fabric for the body of the roll, one 10 x 20in (25 x 50cm) piece of lining, one 10 x 20in (25 x 50cm) piece of interfacing for the pocket and one 10 x 20in (25 x 50cm) piece of wadding.

2 For the pocket, iron the interfacing to the wrong side, fold it in half lengthways and press.

3 Assemble the sandwich: place the wadding on the bottom, the main fabric facing upwards on top, then place the pocket with the folded edge to the middle and the raw edges along the bottom long edge. Place the ribbon on the top right short edge in the centre.

4 Place the second piece of main fabric on top with the wrong side facing upwards. Pin and machine stitch all the way around the edges, leaving a 2in (5cm) opening at the centre top edge for turning. Trim the edges and clip the corners (see page 18).

5 Turn right side out and press. Using a sewing needle and thread, close the opening with slipstitch (see page 15). Using a sewing machine, topstitch (see page 16) all around the side and top edges.

6 Using a disappearing fabric marker or tailor's chalk and ruler, mark vertical lines across the inside of the roll from left to right, in increments of approximately $1^1/2$in (4cm)/$1^1/2$in (4cm)/1in (2.5cm)/1in (2.5cm)/$1^1/2$in (4cm)/$1^1/2$ (4cm)/1in (2.5cm)/1in (2.5cm)/2in (5cm)/2in (5cm)/1in (2.5cm)/$1^1/2$in (4cm)/$1^1/2$in (4cm).

7 Machine stitch along the marked lines, starting at the lower pocket edges and ending at the upper edge, backstitching to secure each end.

Tip

Why not make another roll for your make-up? Mascara, tubes of foundation and lipstick fit wonderfully into the pockets and it prevents everything falling to the bottom of your bag where you can never find it!

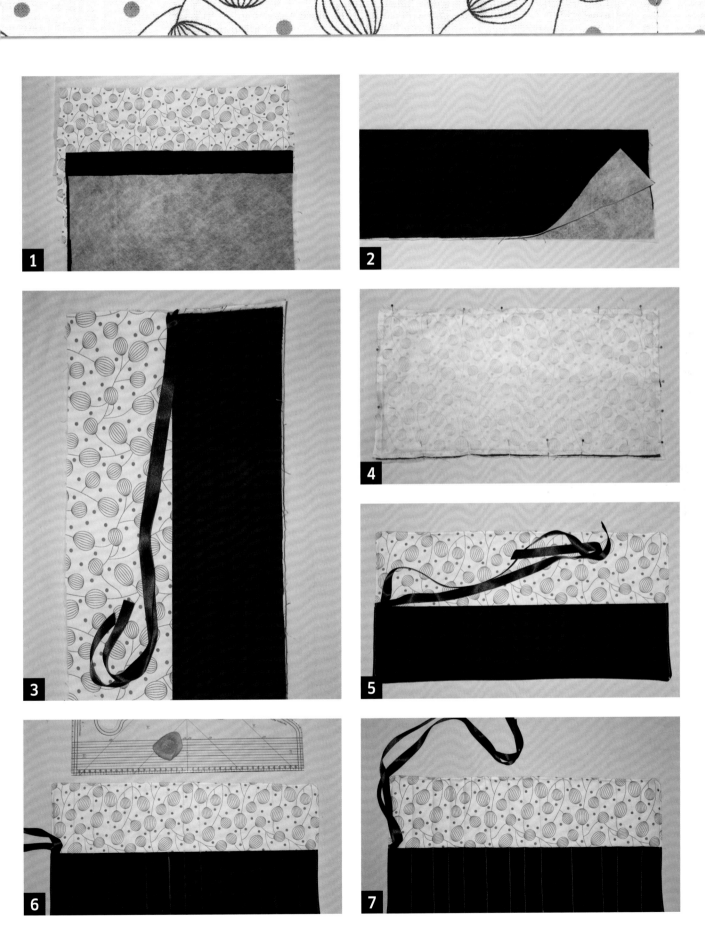

NURSERY

TOY RABBIT

This sweet little rabbit toy has a very simple shape but it is brought to life with brightly coloured felt and a few easy embroidery stitches. It's a quick, simple make that is sure to become a well-loved friend. For even more cuddle appeal, it can be made from fleece.

Finished size is roughly:
5½in (14cm) wide at base x 11in (28cm) high

Find the templates on pages 134–5

You will need
1 fat quarter of fabric
Fusible interfacing
Small amount of contrast felt
Polyester toy stuffing
Embroidery needle and contrast embroidery thread
Sewing needle
Matching thread
Dressmaking scissors and small scissors
Pins
Disappearing fabric marker
Tape measure
Iron/ironing board

NOTE: Felt is one of my favourite fabrics to work with. It never frays, and comes in a wide range of colours that you can use as a contrast or to tone into your project. It is very versatile – use it for appliqué or as the main fabric on a toy or purse and either hand stitch with embroidery thread or use zigzag stitch on the sewing machine.

Tip
A squirt of fabric adhesive will prevent the felt pieces from moving while you sew them in place, without the need for pins.

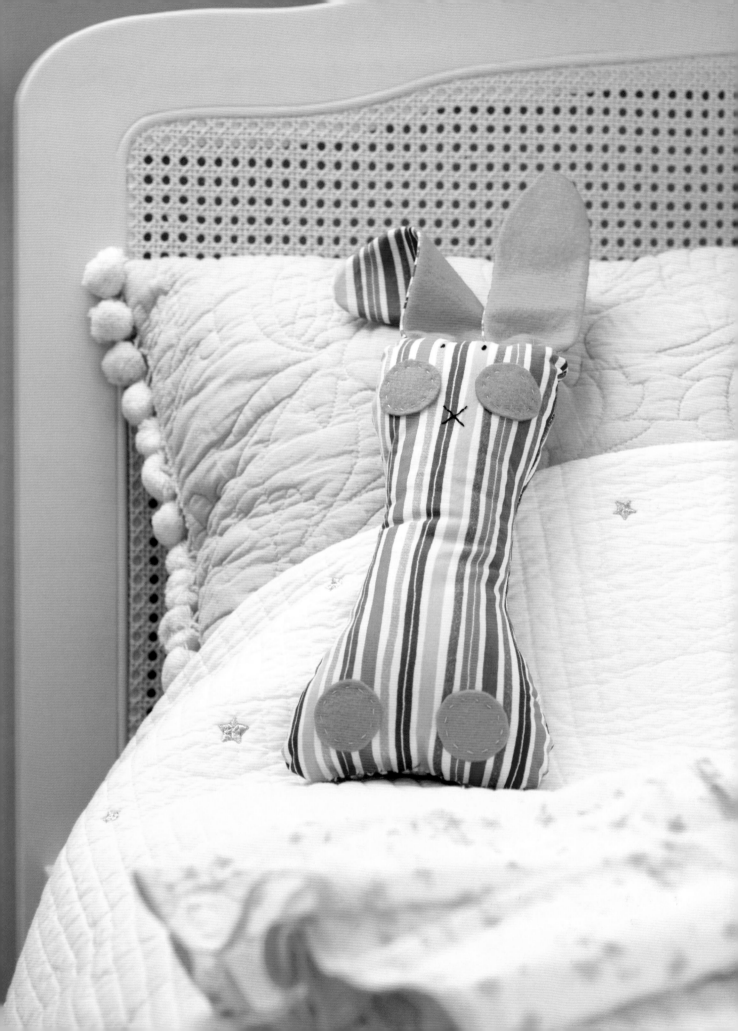

1 Using the templates on pages 134–5, cut out two pieces in main fabric and two pieces in interfacing for the body. For the ears, cut two pieces in main fabric and two pieces in felt. Cut four circles in felt.

2 Assemble the ears. With right sides facing, place one piece of main fabric and one piece of felt together. Pin and machine stitch around the long sides. Turn right side out and press. Repeat for the second ear.

3 Using an embroidery needle and contrast thread, sew a line of running stitches (see page 14) at the base of each ear. Draw up the excess material to make a gather. Secure with a few small stitches and cut the thread.

4 Iron the interfacing to the wrong sides of both body pieces. On one body piece, pin the felt circles to each cheek and, using an embroidery needle and contrast thread, attach them by hand sewing a circle of running stitches just inside the outer edge. Now do the same for the feet, attaching the felt to the lower edge about ¾in (2cm) up from the lower edge.

5 Mark the face with a disappearing fabric marker and, using contrasting embroidery thread and needle, make a cross for the mouth using two long stitches and embroider the eyes using small back stitches (see page 16).

6 Assemble your rabbit by placing the front body onto a flat surface with right side facing upwards. Place the bottom of both ears at the top of the rabbit's head with the tips facing down to its feet. Place the bottom body piece on top of the sandwich with wrong side facing upwards. Pin in place and machine stitch around all the edges using a ⅜in (1cm) seam and leaving the flat lower edge open for turning and stuffing.

7 Turn the rabbit right side out and stuff firmly. When stuffing, work in small batches, filling out the shape as you go. Keep checking you have pushed all the filling into the nooks and crannies before adding more – use the blunt end of a knitting needle to push the wadding into small corners. When happy with the finish and the firmness of the stuffing, pin the lower edges of the fabric inwards and, using needle and matching thread, slipstitch (see page 15) the opening closed.

Tip

If you hate hand sewing, you could always machine stitch the felt pieces in place. A nice zigzag stitch would add to the interest of the face.

1 Fold the material in half and lay the templates on top. In this way you will cut a front and back piece of each shape. Cut one moon shape, two star shapes and two cloud shapes.

2 For the moon and star shapes, place them together with right sides facing and machine around all edges, leaving a 1in (2.5cm) opening for turning. For the cloud shape, place the fabric right side upwards. Cut different lengths and colours of ribbons and pin them to the straight lower edge with the ribbon facing inwards. Place the second piece on top, making sure the ribbon ends are tucked inside. Pin and machine stitch around all edges, leaving a 1in (2.5cm) opening for turning on the top side edge.

3 Turn each shape right side out and stuff firmly. Using a sewing needle and matching thread, close the opening with a few small slipstitches (see page 15).

4 Wrap the silver ribbon around the hoop until it's completely covered. Secure in place with a few small stitches.

5 Cut 5 x 40in (1m) lengths of silver cord. Thread onto a large-eyed needle and make a secure knot at the end. Draw the needle through each shape from bottom to top until the knot sits at the bottom. Attach to the hoop evenly around the edges by wrapping the tail end over the lip and tying with a tight knot. This bit is fiddly so you might need another pair of hands to hold the hoop while you play about with the lengths you want. Try to vary the lengths for more interest.

6 Take the excess cords up to a point above the hoop. Again, you may need another pair of hands to hold things so you can balance the mobile and ensure it hangs straight. Tie all the cord ends together into a knot and trim the excess. Tie lengths of coloured ribbon around the hoop and let it hang.

Tip

A second pair of hands is very helpful when it comes to stringing the mobile. You can add extra interest to the cords by stringing beads to them or adding coloured pompoms, too.

1

2

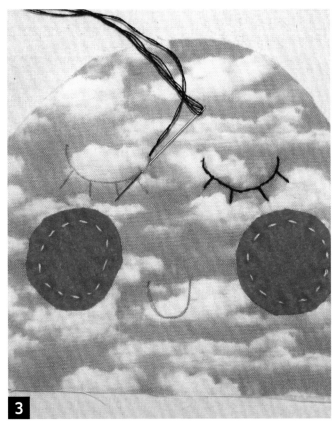

3

4

5

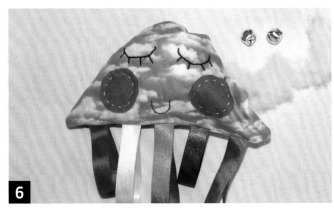

6

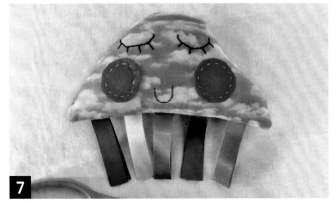

7

DOORSTOP

This cute mouse doorstop will keep the nursery door ajar in style. Add whiskers, eyes and rosy felt cheeks, plus anything else you like, to the mouse's face. These touches will add character and individuality to the project. Use lentils or rice to weigh it down.

Finished size is roughly:
4½in (12cm) wide at base x 8in (20cm) high

Find the templates on page 139

You will need
1 fat quarter of fabric
Small pieces of contrasting felt
1 bead for nose
1lb (500g) pack of lentils or rice for stuffing
Polyester toy stuffing
Sewing needle and matching thread
Sewing machine
Dressmaking scissors
Paper-cutting scissors
Pins
Disappearing fabric marker
Iron and ironing board

NOTE: If you don't have a bead for the nose, a small pompom would look just as good.

Tip

This project is so cute it would also look fabulous hung on the wall in a nursery! This can easily be achieved by using stuffing instead of the rice or lentils and adding a little loop at the back to hang over a wall hook.

1 Using the templates on page 139, cut your base circle and body pieces out from your fabric.

2 With right sides together, machine stitch both curved side seams on the body pieces.

3 With right sides together, pin the base circle halfway around your body piece. Machine stitch the pinned half of the circle using a ³⁄₈in (1cm) seam allowance.

4 Turn the doorstop right side out and begin stuffing. Use polyester toy filling for the top part of the doorstop, moulding the nose as you go. When you have stuffed halfway down, add the bag of lentils or rice. Add extra stuffing around the bag.

5 Pin the remaining half of the base in place and, using a needle and matching thread, slipstitch (see page 15) the remaining opening firmly closed.

6 Using the templates, cut out the ear pieces from the felt. Place the smaller part of the felt ear inside the larger felt part. Using contrasting embroidery thread and a running stitch (see page 14), work around the inside of the smaller felt piece. Pinch the lower part in half and hand stitch firmly to one side of the mouse's head. Repeat for the second ear.

7 Sew the mouse's nose firmly in place using a sewing needle and thread. Cut a thin strip of contrasting felt for the tail and hand stitch that firmly in place to its rear end.

Tip

To avoid the mess and fiddle of pouring loose lentils or rice into the body, first place them into a strong, sealable plastic bag and insert it into the doorstop.

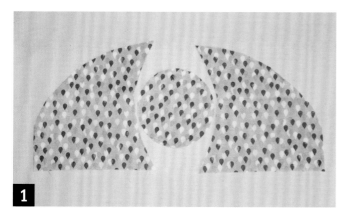

1

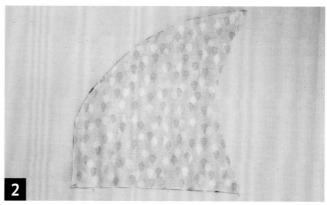

2

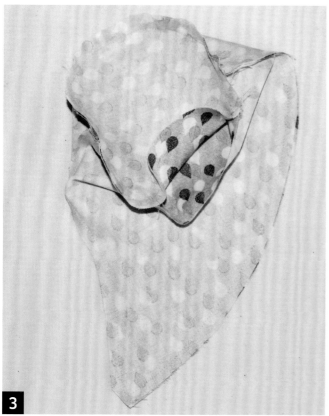

3

4

5

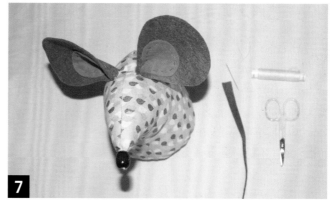

6

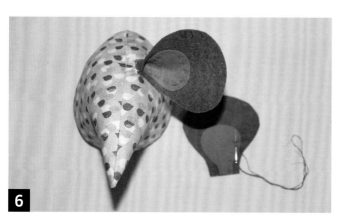

7

COMFORTER

My daughter loved her comforter and took it everywhere with her. This loveable teddy bear definitely has the cuddle factor with the softest fleece body, which is perfect for snuggling up with. His sweet, sleepy face gives him plenty of character.

Finished size is roughly:
10½in (27cm) wide x 15in (38cm) high

Find the templates on page 140

You will need
1 fat quarter of fleece fabric
Small amount of felt
Polyester toy stuffing
Embroidery needle and contrast embroidery thread
Sewing needle and matching thread
Pins
Tape measure
Dressmaking scissors
Small sharp scissors
Sewing machine
Disappearing fabric marker

NOTE: Fleece can be tricky to work with, as it sheds fibres once cut and also blunts fabric scissors and sewing-machine needles. Be sure to sharpen your scissors after cutting the fleece, and replace the needle in your machine after sewing, too. Make sure to adjust the presser foot of your machine to its highest setting to accommodate the bulk.

Tip
Change the needle on your sewing machine to a ballpoint needle when sewing fleece to make it easier, and clean your machine afterwards.

1 For the bear's body, cut two squares of fur fleece 14 x 14in (36 x 36cm).

2 The fur has a right side and a wrong side i.e. a fluffy side and a more matt one. Place the right sides (the fluffy sides) together and machine stitch around all the edges using a 5/8in (1.5cm) seam allowance and leaving a 2in (5cm) opening for turning. Trim the excess fur, turn right side out and close the opening with a few small slipstitches (see page 15) using matching thread.

3 For the ears, first cut out the two felt ear pieces using the template then place the felt ear piece straight onto a small square of fleece and machine stitch all around the curved edges using a 1/4in (6mm) seam. Leave the bottom seam open for turning later. Repeat for the second ear.

4 Trim the excess fur and turn right side out.

5 Cut out the two felt head pieces using the template on page 140 in your main colour of felt. To assemble the head, first place the bear's face onto a flat surface facing upwards. Place the ears on top of the head, one on each side of the centre point and facing inwards, with the open seam matched with the outer edge of the face piece. Place the back part of the head on top of the sandwich and pin. Machine stitch around the edge using a 3/8in (1cm) seam allowance and leaving a 1in (2.5cm) opening below the bear's chin for turning. Turn right side out and stuff firmly with polyester toy filling. Using a sewing needle and matching thread, close the opening on the bear's head using a firm slipstitch. Position the bear's head in the centre of the fleece square and hand stitch in place under the chin.

6 Using a disappearing fabric marker, mark the bear's features and, with an embroidery needle and contrast thread, use small backstitches (see page 16) to fill in the mouth and eyes.

7 Lay out the fur body and cut the tummy piece using the template on page 140. Stitch in place to the centre of the body using a sewing needle, contrast embroidery thread and a line of running stitch (see page 14) just inside the outer edge.

8 Place the head above the tummy piece at the centre point of the fur body. Pin in place, turn over and, using a sewing needle and matching thread, backstitch firmly in place.

9 For the paws, measure up about 2in (5cm) from each corner point of the body and, using a sewing needle and matching thread, use small running stitches across the diagonal and draw tight to make each paw. Take the needle through the gathers several times before securing in place with a few small stitches.

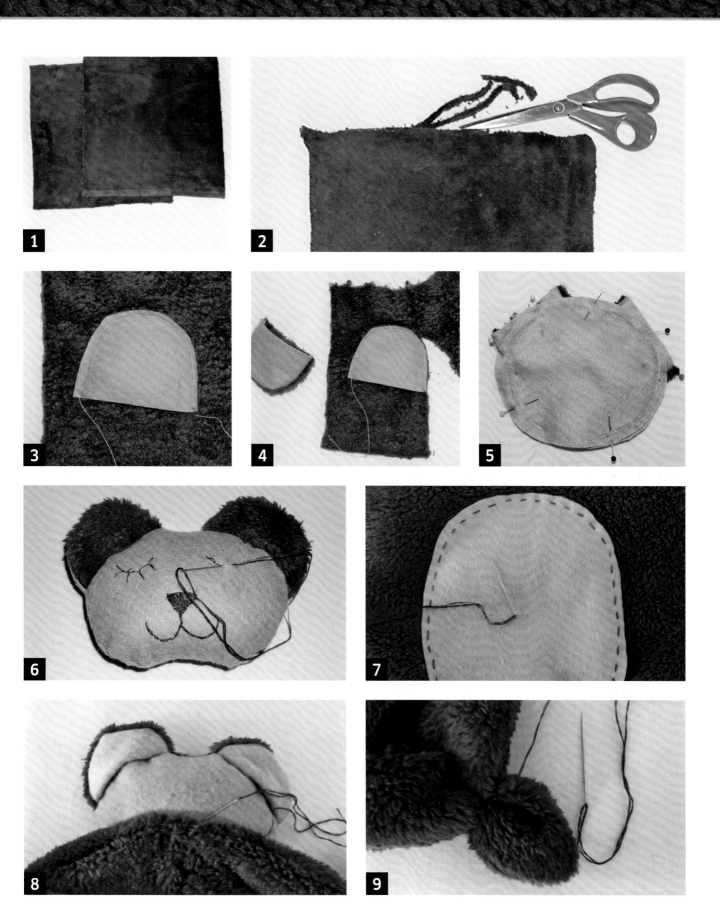

TEMPLATES

Templates that are shown
at actual size can be
traced and cut out, or
photocopied. For templates
that have been reduced
in size, enlarge them on
an A3 photocopier to the
percentage stated.

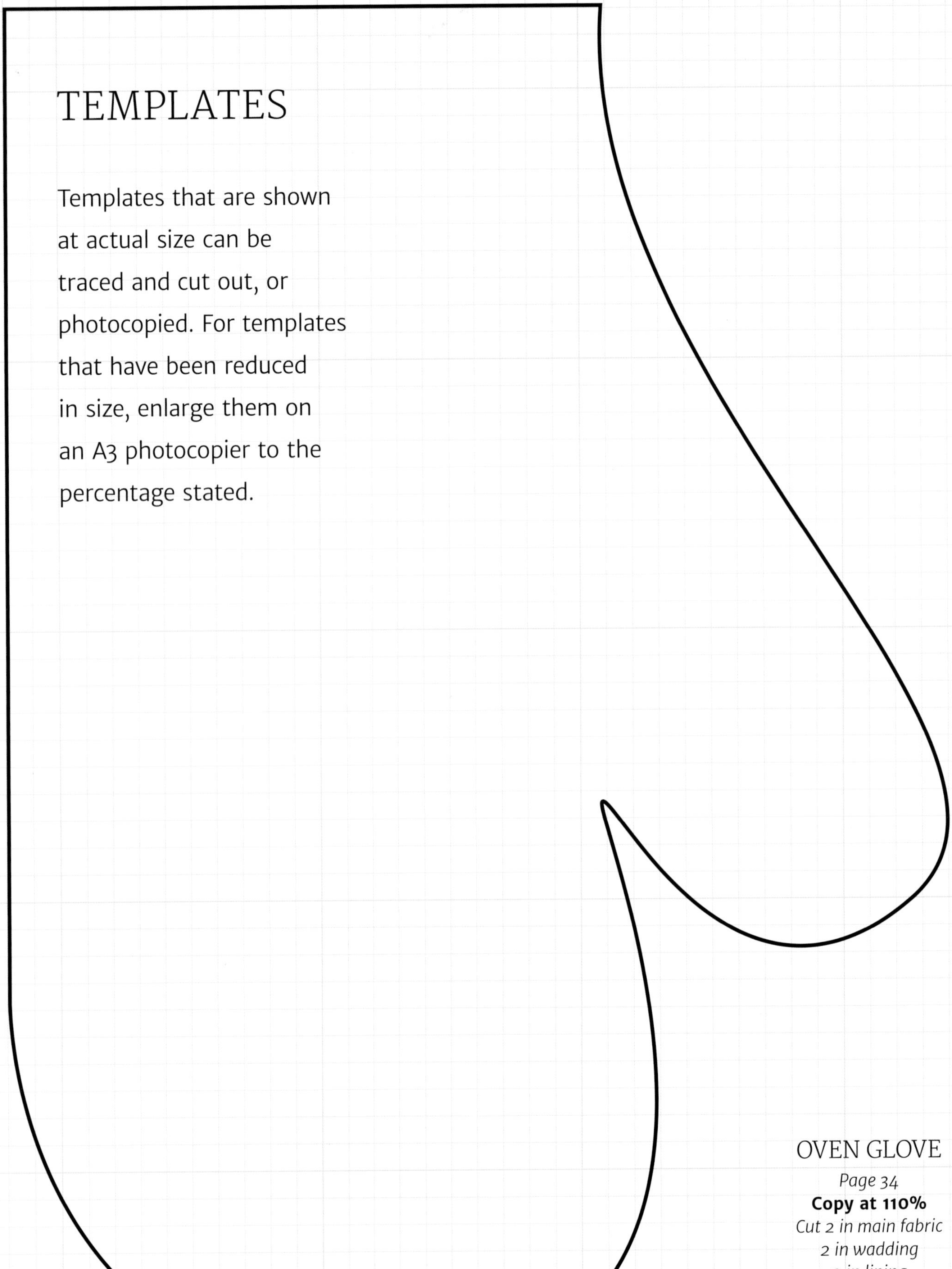

OVEN GLOVE
Page 34
Copy at 110%
*Cut 2 in main fabric
2 in wadding
2 in lining*

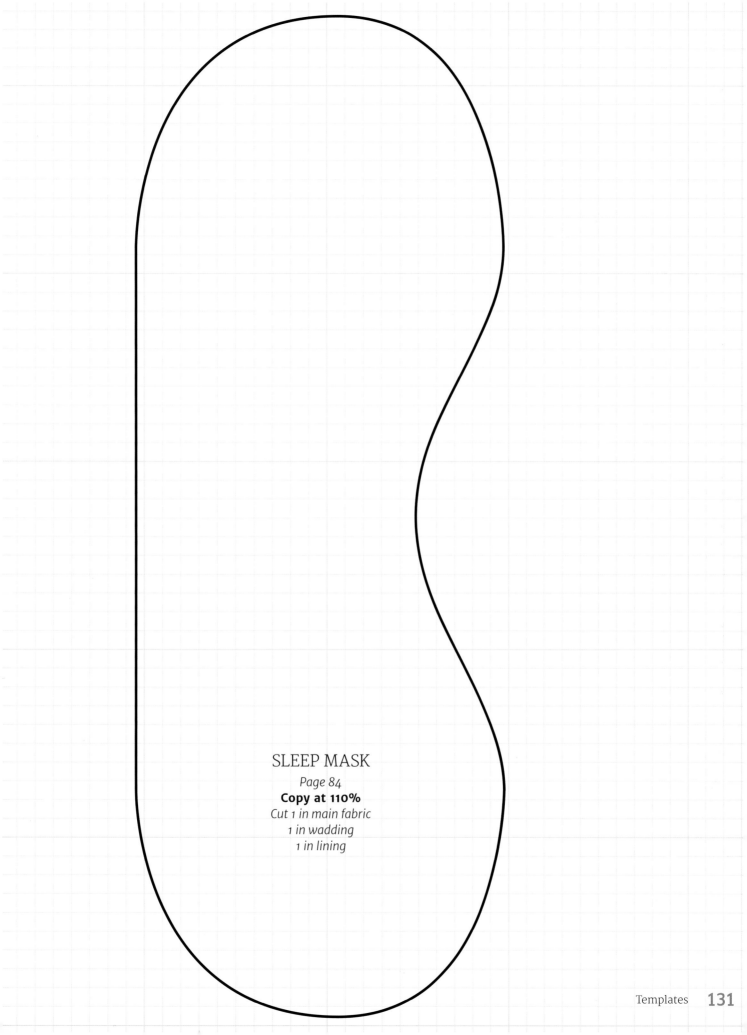

SLEEP MASK

Page 84
Copy at 110%
*Cut 1 in main fabric
1 in wadding
1 in lining*

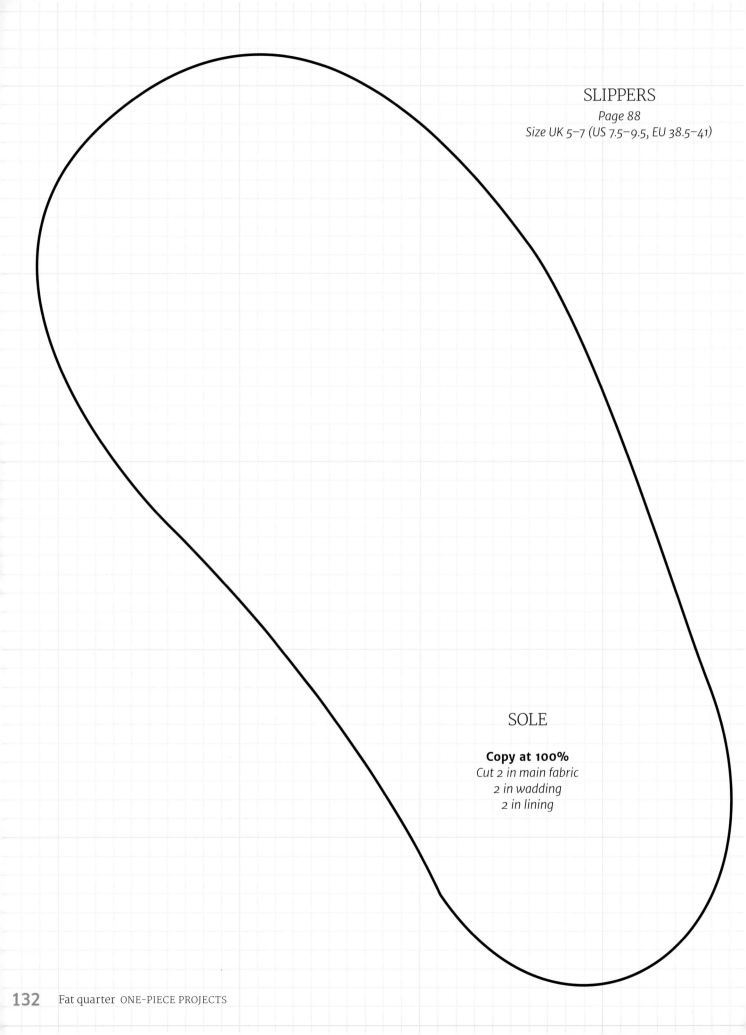

SLIPPERS

Page 88
Size UK 5–7 (US 7.5–9.5, EU 38.5–41)

SOLE

Copy at 100%
Cut 2 in main fabric
2 in wadding
2 in lining

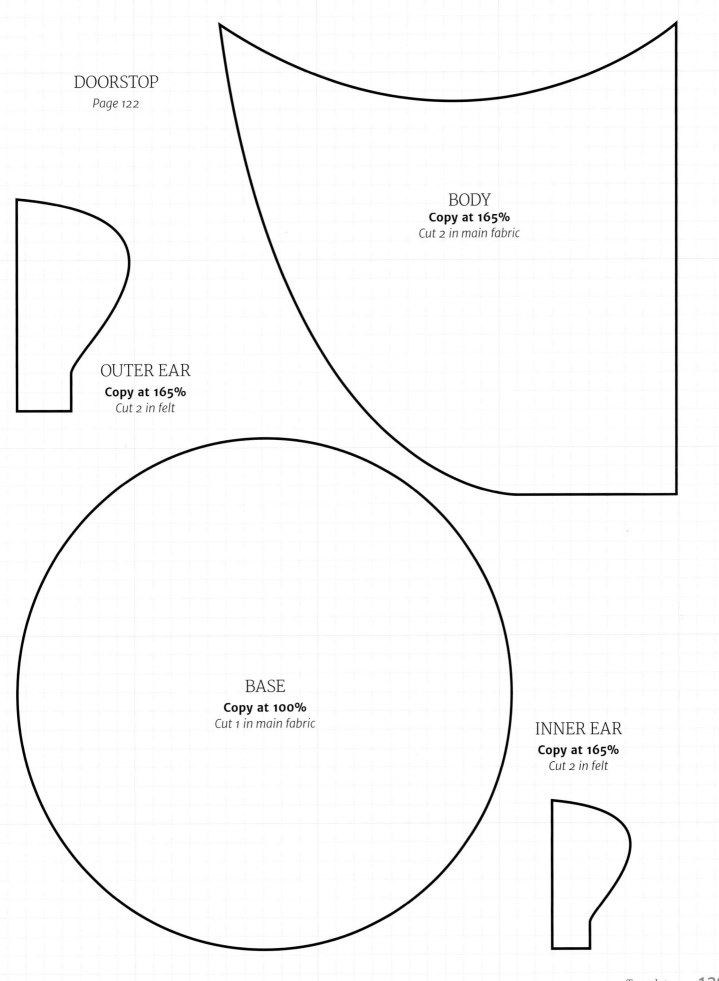

DOORSTOP
Page 122

BODY
Copy at 165%
Cut 2 in main fabric

OUTER EAR
Copy at 165%
Cut 2 in felt

BASE
Copy at 100%
Cut 1 in main fabric

INNER EAR
Copy at 165%
Cut 2 in felt

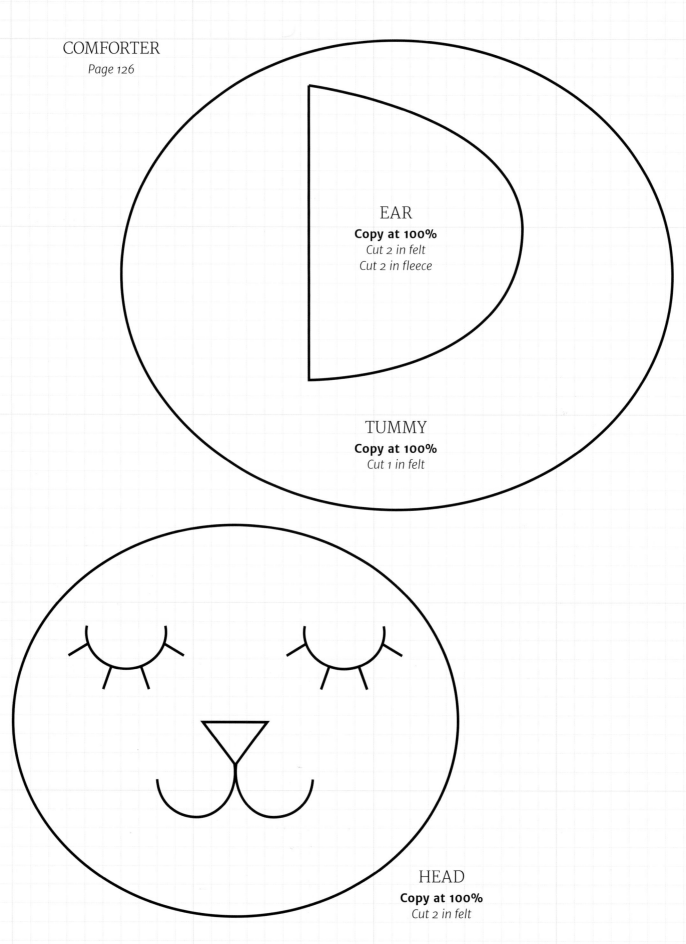

COMFORTER

Page 126

EAR

Copy at 100%

Cut 2 in felt

Cut 2 in fleece

TUMMY

Copy at 100%

Cut 1 in felt

HEAD

Copy at 100%

Cut 2 in felt

RESOURCES

Fabric & quilting supplies
www.sewinspiredplymouth.co.uk

Scissors
www.fiskars.co.uk

Embroidery thread
www.dmc.com/uk/

Fusible webbing, interfacing,
fabrics & haberdashery
www.craft-box.com

ACKNOWLEDGEMENTS

Big thanks to all at GMC Publications Ltd, especially Jonathan, Dominique
and Gilda for helping me fulfill the original vision and also for making
the book so beautiful. Special thanks also goes to my photographer Jeff,
who wrestled with the UK's temperamental natural winter light to make
the step-by-step photos as clear and perfect as possible. Also, thank you
to Julie at Sew Inspired Plymouth, who let me photograph endless bolts
of fabric so I would have the perfect one for each project, and to Liz from
Painters in Liskeard. Your haberdashery selection is faultless. To my
family, sorry. You can have the kitchen table back. Meals on laps are now
officially over!

GMC Publications would like to thank: Ruby and Harvey Sellens for
modelling; Anna Stevens for providing the location for the shoot;
and Wayne Blades for the photography styling.

INDEX

To order a book, or to request
a catalogue, contact:

GMC Publications Ltd
Castle Place, 166 High Street,
Lewes, East Sussex,
BN7 1XU
United Kingdom
Tel: +44 (0)1273 488005
www.gmcbooks.com